Prologue

Before there were Gods,

there was one Goddess Blue,

and out of the blue she blew

a bubble of light

into the indigo night

and created the Glamours in her hue.

On starlight they came

on that indigo night.

There are 9 of them in all

and they are your guides.

For they hold a mystery within their midsts.

To hear of this mystery

is to experience bliss.

Now to find their realm is a doorway

you'll see,

opened through the 4 Elements

and the magic of Glamoury.

E&R

PUBLISHERS OF O.G. AUTHOR GENIUSES

Written, designed, and created by Kim Bieber
Copyright © 2023
All rights reserved.

ISBN: 9781945674693
Library of Congress Catalog Card Number: 2023932752
Published by E&R, New York

Glamoury

Transform yourself and get the look of Glamoury

Glamour and Beauty

Glamoury is a system of beauty that emanates from the goddess on the blue star of Sirius. There are nine Glamours who each hold a piece of her celestial wisdom, and they have been known throughout time by different names. In Egypt, they were called the Ennead. In India, they became known as the Navadurgas. In ancient Greece, they were the Muses, and in Britain, the Ladies of the Lake. By any name, the Glamours are agents of change who bring about transformation by revealing the goddess within.

Glamour and Magic

In ancient times, the word glamour (gramarye) meant magic. In legend, to be 'in glamour' was to dwell among the fairies and elementals in the otherworldly realm of the goddess. Some say this queendom is what the knights quested and the Ladies of the Lake (the Glamours of the time) protected. Entering this realm was a journey often beset with challenges because to enter into pure beauty, one must first recognize what is truly beautiful.

In today's world, the word glamour has lost some of its mystical origin. Yet access to its magic is more available than ever before. This is because the goddess is no longer a riddle. She is a state of being for both men and women to create within. However, to be empowered by her magic, the alchemical journey to beauty remains the same. One must quest for the true self and transform what is inauthentic into gold. One way to do this is through color, shape, and texture by wearing fashion that corresponds to your element.

Air Water Fire Earth

There are four elements: AIR, WATER, FIRE, and EARTH. Each element has its own shapes, colors, textures, and ways of moving and being. You are a combination of all the elements, but one predominates in your appearance. This is the element for you to wear because it enhances the most positive qualities within you.

By enhancing your most positive qualities, you will move beyond trends that might not be you and amplify your truth. This amplification will have the effect of casting out all that is inauthentic, as truth is always more powerful than performance.

In your element, you will also find it becomes easy to let go of what hides you, depletes you, and causes disharmony around you. As you do this, you will lighten, and your beauty will show.

Vibrational Cosmology

The traditional way to choose color and style has been to consider eye color, skin tone, body shape, and mood. In recent times, there have also been seasons of the year to choose from, determined by a stylist or friend. But there is another method that has yet to be revealed, and it is done through numerology.

In numerology, each letter in the alphabet corresponds to a specific number. When you add up the numbers in your name, you receive your essence number. This number is your signature vibration. It is the frequency you resonate with, and just like your name introduces your spirit, your essence number introduces how you move, think, and feel.

The essence number has many components to discover. But what is important in Glamoury is the element it corresponds to—this element you carry with you throughout your life. Even if you change your name, the element you were born with remains the same. It is like your sun sign in astrology. It is a doorway to who you are.

How It Works

To find your element, add together the numbers of your first, middle, and last name as found on your birth certificate. The name on your birth certificate is important because that is your original frequency.

Use the number table to find the value of each letter in your name.

You can also visit glamoury.com, and the element calculator will add it for you.

1 2 3 4 5 6 7 8
A B C D E U O F
I K G M H V Z P
Q R L T N W
J S X
Y

Follow the example below to find your element.

You will be reducing your name to a single number between one and

nine, with the exception of 11 and 22.

Kimberly Dean Bieber

2+1+4+2+5+2+3+1+4+5+1+5+2+1+5+2+5+2=61

Reduce 61 by adding 6+1 which equals 7.

6+1=7

7 is the element of Water

If your number is greater than 9, reduce it again unless it is 11 or 22.

For example 10 is 1+0=1.

1 is the element of Fire.

1. Fire

2. Earth

3. Fire

4. Earth

5. Air

6. Air

7. Water

8. Earth

9. Fire

11. Air

22. Water

Wearing Your Element

Now that you have discovered your element, it is time to be in it. On the following pages, each element and how to wear it is explained. As you move through the journey of Glamoury, you will also notice there are keywords. These words define the message each element brings. When you wear your element, these words will become a part of you and emanate around you like perfume.

The way this works is similar to how an opera singer can shatter a glass by singing a note equal to the frequency of the glass. When you wear your element's colors and styles, you are matching its frequency to you. This raises your vibration to a higher level and allows what is already beautiful within you to show.

However, over time, you can—and you will want to combine the other elements—as Glamoury is not a rigid system. Glamoury is alchemy, and alchemy works by bringing something precious out of the darkness and into the light.

Now take your number and let the Glamours guide you through the elements to the beauty within you.

At the top of the mountain you will breath the clear fresh Air that will set you free!

Air

Carefree

Youthful *Independent*

5, 6, & 11 are those who are AIR.
They bring light and inspiration to all who seek what's fair.
Bright bubbles create butterflies to be your guides
                        to the celadon light in the sky.
For the Crystal People are those from whom you came,
            they are translucent blue starlight
            and come home in spring.
Dissolve yourself in their chrysalis of light,
            re-emerge brighter and ready to take flight.

Original

Bubbly *Air* *Charming*

Air is the element of innovation, inspiration, and lightness.
It carries with it the possibility of new ideas, effervescence, and fun.
People who are Air are lively friends and progressive thinkers.
They are like butterflies,
colorful, bright, and lovely to behold.
If Air is your element, you like to think outside of the box.
It is your nature to allow your creativity to overflow.
Your presence makes others feel at ease.
However, know that too much bubbly Air can cause you confusion and doubt.

If you are attracted to Air, but it is not your element, use its qualities to break
inertia and enter into the airy realm of ideas.
Invoke the style of Air to set yourself free.

Your colors range from the amber honey of the bee, to
the coral reefs in the aqua sea.

Pastel

Dewey

Flaxen

Crisp

Bright

Air

To allow the beauty of Air to show,
begin by wearing its sunshine colors closest to your face.
Good choices are chamomile, white daisy, iris blue, and petal pink.
As a highlight, apply a lip gloss in a light tone.
Air complexion has a honey finish over a natural pastel base,
therefore peaches and cream colors will set you aglow.
To find the colors of Air in nature, look to the pastel flowers of Spring.
Spring is a time of new beginnings when the caterpillar turns
into a butterfly and lets itself go.

Delicate

Sassy

Animated

Fun

Effervescent

Playful

Your shapes
are free
and fun
and bright.
Inspiring
others
with
your
lightness
is
your
might.

Air

The rhythm of Air is upward, outward, and diffuse.
It moves like a butterfly and symbolizes spreading joy, love, and peace.
To be in harmony with this rhythm,
wear higher hemlines and necklines that keep you afloat.
Patterns such as plaids, stripes, ginghams, and tiny florals
will let your true feelings show.
The animated textures found on eyelet,
seersucker, fine wale courdoroy
and boucle will make you feel bright.
Blue jeans and a tee-shirts
make an Airy outfit.
Add a decal
or sequins
for an extra sassy feel.

Air

How to Wear Air

Air energy is effervescent and light.
Air people go through life and
accomplish their goals in this way.
If you are Air, make sure your
fashion coveys this buoyancy.
To bring it all together, style your
hair to be in sync with this rhythm.
A ponytail, wisps, curls, or a pair of
fun clips are a good start.

Pants

Air pants are best cut at the waist. Low-waisted trousers are acceptable if your shirt uplifts the energy. Pant lines for Air are varied and can be straight, wide, or boot cut. Flared pants might drag you down, but stripes will send the energy back up. Make sure your fabric conveys a lightness. If you need warmth, try a light wool fabric in your colors.

Jackets & Coats

Baseball jackets and down puffers are Air. The tuck at the waist gives them a buoyant appearance. Cropped dress jackets and denim jackets also lift the energy up. Try your jackets in a stippled sear sucker or a polka-dot pattern for an extra bubbly appearance. Winter coats that are long and warm should still look light. A rounded collar will create an Airy look.

Shoes

Air shoes have round ballet toes or dainty and delicate points.
A confetti bow or sequins will help highlight the effervescence of your shoe.
Bright stripes add fun to tennis shoes.
Flip flops in your colors are an easy-going choice.
On the heavier side, cowboy boots with floral appliques are Air.
As are many knee-high zipper boots in your sassy colors.

Shirts

Air shirts are light and casual and often frilly.
Bows, sequins, pearls, and ruffles can all adorn an Air shirt.
A sweetheart neckline will convey your innocence.
A round or v-neck tee can be great fun.
The key to Air is lightness, so pick shirts that make you feel carefree.
Deeper necklines, which tend to be Water, can be worn with a short necklace
to pull the energy up.

Skirts

Mini skirts, prairie skirts, and flounced skirts are Air.
Gathers, runching, pleats, tiers, and petticoats create an inspirational look.
Fabric is essential. Make sure it's light.
Eyelet and lace are excellent choices.
When wearing heavier skirts, texture, and pattern will uplift the weight.

Purses & Bags

A petite clutch in an active and inspiring pattern creates a light appearance. Large adornments, such as buckles, will weigh you down. The light texture of a straw tote will be a fresh addition to your outfit. Add an appliqué for fun.

Take this cup wherever you go.
Drink from this elixir
and follow your heart home.

WATER

Mysterious   *Sensitive*

    Resourceful   *Compassionate*

Intuitive   *Generous*

7 & 22

are the Water that flows from the heart,
   into soft subtle mists on an ocean of summer light.
Part these mists and dive deep into lands unknown,
    where the dolphins are your guides
      and the Crystal Castle is your home.
For the Dolphin People are those from whom you came,
   to love and give direction to all who seek their way.
   Dive deep, dive deep, then come up for air.
Blow your bubbles of violet light into the world we share.

Water

Water has a natural grace and effortless flow. It represents compassion, and people who are Water have much in common with the dolphins of the seas. Like the dolphins, Water people find strength in their community. They are resilient and intuit the subtle undercurrents in situations.

If Water is your element, you tend to feel deeply. Like rivers that carve grand canyons, your power is in your current.
Keep in mind that your greatest enemy is stagnation. When you feel the waters cease to flow, look to your heart and follow it home.

If you are seeking Water, but it is not your element, you may be looking for gratitude, empathy, and connection. To harness this energy, reflect upon its keywords and let your dolphin-sense guide you to these depths.

Your colors range from the deepest blue of the sea, to the softest seashell pink,
and the purple velvet of a dark summer night's breeze.

Soft

Subtle

Muted

Misty

Tranquil

Calm

Water

To allow the beauty of Water to flow, wear soothing colors
that make you feel unrestricted.
Dusty rose, taupe, soft grey and blues that blend into the
moonlight are good choices to begin.
Water people have cool skin with a rosy undertone,
so be aware that brassy colors will drown you out.

To find the colors of Water in nature, look to the seashore in summer.
In summer, the flowers are open, and the trees are in full bloom.
Everything is settled, sensitive, ripe, and whole.

Nurturing

Pretty

Relaxed

Flowing

Blended

Draping

Long

Open and flow into the world around you.
Relax into your style and let the water surround you.

Water

Water people move like dolphins,
and their nature is to dive deep.
To reflect this rhythm in your style,
wear your hemlines long, and your pant lines flared.
Let your necklines flow without sharp collars, points,
or heavy jewelry.
Always feel your fabrics for softness
because of all the elements in Glamoury,
Water relies on feeling the most.

Water

HOW TO WEAR WATER

Water energy is cool and flowing, and it moves around obstacles to reach its goal. If you are Water, make sure your fashion conveys this rhythm. To bring it all together, blend from head to toe and avoid clothing that restricts you.

WATER

SKIRTS

The key to Water skirts is how they move. Water skirts need flow and grace. Hemlines that drape below the knee are best. Long slits that make you feel pretty are a grand choice. Skirts with pleats, gathers, and runching can be worn. But too many ruffles, tiers, and gathers will agitate your soft appearance.

SHOES

Water shoes are soft and flexible. Lower heels will feel best as Water flows down, not up. Toes that are oval, not pointed, will make you feel comfortable. Straps should have a nice graceful curve. The color of your shoe should blend with your outfit. Avoid the sharpness of pointy stilettos and the heaviness of boxy heels.

PURSES & HANDBAGS

Shoulder bags and handbags are a vital aspect of the Water appearance. They should be soft, supple, and blend in with your outfit. Avoid contrasting colors, oversized buckles, rivets, or too much topstitching. A subtle purse in soft suede or leather is a more appropriate choice and will add drape instead of weight to your outfit.

SHIRTS

Water necklines are deep and oval. Dress shirts look best when fitted but not tight. Turtlenecks should cascade, and sleeves should fall gently toward the wrist. Avoid shoulder pads or any style that uplifts the energy. Choose a flowing tunic in one of your colors instead.

PANTS

Water pants have long graceful lines, and flare will convey movement. Avoid zig-zags, noticeable buttons, and appliques, as they will agitate you. Check the shapes of the pockets. Prominent pockets aren't the best. Denim should be very soft. Wear a longer shirt to cover the waistline if there are too many buttons and loops.

JACKETS & COATS

A long coat that conveys ease is a watery choice. Business jackets are best worn not too short, with a graceful line at the collar and waist. Avoid prominent buttons, pointy collars, boxy pockets, and straight lines. Baseball jackets or any item that gathers too tightly at the waist will cut your outfit in half. Overly weighty coats may drag you down.

WATER

IGNITE YOUR COURAGE
AND YOU WILL SEE
THE BLAZING SOUL
YOU ARE MEANT TO BE.

FIRE

1, 3, & 9

are Fire who refract the light.

    Bringing the brightness of day into the night.

For the Phoenix People are those from whom you came;

    they bubbled out of the volcano to create again.

Follow their cyan blue, the hottest part of the flame,

    and you will fly higher,

        more direct

    and return whence you came.

DYNAMIC   ENCOURAGING

SELF ASSURED   IN COMMAND

COURAGEOUS   INTENSE

ENERGETIC   # FIRE

Fire is a driving force that gets things done.

It is the element of dynamic aspirations, initiative, and vitality.

People who are Fire are tried and true.

Like the mythical phoenix, they are able to fly ever higher

and reinvent themselves again and again.

If Fire is your element, you radiate courage and leadership.

The warmth of your personality attracts many admirers and friends.

Of all the elements in Glamoury, Fire communicates the essence of freedom.

Yet people of this element also like to be in command.

So to hold your Fire, don't allow it to burn out of control.

If you are attracted to Fire, but it is not your element,

you may be seeking confidence, courage, and renewal.

If this is the case, use its keywords to connect to your action and will,

for it is within the Fire that you will find your fate.

Your colors range from the mossy green

to the deep umber shades of the fallen autumn leaves.

SOLAR

GOLDEN

BITTERSWEET

RUSTY

STRONG

BRASSY

AUTUMNAL

FIRE

To allow the beauty of Fire to glow, wear solar colors
that embody your emblazoned strength.
If it feels too intense, begin with a terra cotta pink close to your face.
Then add a sheer lipgloss in a cinnamon tone.

Keep in mind that all your colors have a golden and spicy undertone.
Therefore warm ivory, mossy green, turquoise, dijon yellow,
and sienna brown will give you that ember glow.
In nature, the colors of Fire are found in autumn. A time when the
leaves turn a warm reddish-brown hue
as the Fire of the sun moves closer to earth.

Your shapes are pyramids,
diamonds and
angles of light.
Your dynamic energy lifts
those around you
up in flight.

SHARP

    ANGULAR

        ASYMMETRICAL

   SUBSTANTIAL

           TEXTURED   # FIRE

      JAGGED

Fire energy is driven, and people who are Fire move like the phoenix
in a dynamic and angular way.

To set yourself alight,
dare to wear
the motion of asymmetrical necklines and hemlines.
Adding texture, topstitching, rivets, buckles, and beads
will allow the rhythm of the firebird within to show.
Distressed fabrics, animal prints, and textured lace in your colors will
bring it all together. Add some substantial jewelry.

Don't hold back.
Just go for it.

FIRE

HOW TO WEAR FIRE

The rhythm of Fire is self assured, and people who are Fire move through life in a dynamic way. Therefore, Fire fashion is best when it conveys a warmth and determination.

FIRE

SHIRTS

Necklines for Fire are angular, and collars have points.

Epaulets will uplift you.

Rolling up your sleeves will give you an active boost.

Unless you seek to tone down your commanding nature,

be cautious of any shirt that drapes.

If you flip your collar up, the energy of Fire will take off.

SKIRTS

Asymmetrical hemlines will create a dynamic look.

If you choose a plain skirt, fire it up with texture and solar tones.

Pleated skirts with prominent folds are Fire.

Add an animal print to give your outfit the action it deserves.

SHOES

Fire shoes are substantial in texture or weight, or both!

Toes are angular and sharp.

(A wooden shoe with a buckle and top stitching may override a round toe.)

Try it and see!

When wearing a softer shoe, choose something with texture in your colors.

Make sure your high heels are self-assured and make you feel in command.

PANTS

Fire pants should have an angle.

Avoid flowy pants, cropped pants, and boxy trousers.

Heavy top stitching on denim and cargo pockets will add to your appearance.

Fire is the element of courage. Use the motto 'go for it.'

PURSES & BAGS

When it comes to shoulder bags, you can Fire them up and embellish them with gold, copper, beads, buckles, stitching, and prints.

Purses in woven leather or distressed suede will make you feel alive.

Textured crochet works well for lighter bags.

Avoid shiny and boxy briefcases.

Your nature requires a more energetic tote.

JACKETS & COATS

Dress jackets with pointed collars and angular pockets will create a commanding look.

Epaulets will add perfection.

Cable sweaters and wooden buttons will make you feel great.

Sheepskin and all sorts of distressed leathers work well for warmth.

Avoid too much shine, as your dynamic personality requires more substance.

FIRE

Find your purpose and you will be
on a path as sure
as aquamarine.

EARTH

2, 4, & 8

are the Earth you seek.

A solid ground to land on and gaze at the deepest blue sea.

It is the Earth that carries beauty with ease and grace.

Like the snow of winter, there is stillness,

sense of purpose, power, and strength.

For the home of the Earth is the home of us all.

The blue jewel of life on which the cat people make their home.

The first to come here from the ethereal star,

they hold open the marble gateway to travel afar.

STRIKING

DISTINCT

STRAIGHTFORWARD

CONSCIENTIOUS

THEATRICAL

CLEAR

EARTH

Earth is the element of stability, steadfastness, and distinction. Earth people are like true gems, precisely cut and finely tuned. They hold themselves with cat-like poise and move with dignity and refinement.

If Earth is your element, you tend to be very straightforward. You have an innate executive ability to make precise and meaningful decisions. You always like to add a theatrical touch to everything you do. However, know that too much Earth can lead to drama. So be conscious that you remain balanced and do not become cold.

When you wear the shapes and colors of Earth, you will connect to the beauty in refinement. If you seek Earth, but it is not your element, use its qualities to find clarity and direction. Waste no time on inessentials. Be very precise, direct, and clear.

Your colors are as bold as a black and white game of chess.
Like cassis in winter on a clear aquamarine day.

PURE

ICY

PRIMARY

CONTRASTING

VIVID

SHARP

EARTH

Earth colors are clear and cool. Light colors have an icy shimmer. Dark colors are saturated and bold. Wearing the jewel tones of diamond, emerald, sapphire, or ruby will make you look striking. Black and white are worn successfully by those who are Earth.

To allow the beauty of Earth to shine, highlight your clear complexion with frosty tones. Metallics can adorn your clothing and your eyes. Earth corresponds to the season of winter, and you can look to the pure colors found during this time to create your look.

Your shapes are as sure as a snowflake of ice.
Like a gem cut stone,
distinct and smooth and perfectly designed.

BOLD

SLEEK

SMOOTH

GEOMETRIC

STYLIZED

METHODICAL

REFINED

EARTH

Earth energy moves like a cat. Its rhythm has poise, and it is focused on its goal. Therefore the best patterns for Earth are minimal or bold.

As for fabrics, icy synthetics, smooth leathers, and neatly pressed textiles will always make you stand out in a crowd. Hemlines and necklines will support you when they are theatrical or distinct. The drama of Earth likes opposites, so contrast will make you feel at ease.

Keep in mind Earth always conveys a still and organized appearance. So avoid drape, wrinkles, and bagginess even in your hairstyle.

EARTH

HOW TO WEAR EARTH

'Refined and Defined' is your keynote. The least amount of agitation, the more stable your appearance will be. The rhythm of Earth is very methodical. It is sure of itself. So build your look with discretion.

EARTH

SHIRTS

Necklines for Earth have geometry. Geometric shapes are square, round, rectangle, and triangle. Earth wears these primary forms because they have poise and structure. The classic tee is Earth, as long as it is clean and neat. Synthetic shirts with shiny metallic threads will make you feel like a star. A white dress shirt is straight up your alley.

SKIRTS

Earth skirts are sleek and smooth, and straight. They are not "earthy." They are precise. All lengths are acceptable as long as the form has structure. Structure means your skirt has a clear and definite shape. Prairie skirts with too many frills and flounces are not your style. A tailored skirt in a bold retro pattern will look more chic.

SHOES

The toes of your shoes are best in a primary shape. Buckles should have geometry. High heels with straps above the ankle, perhaps with a contrasting clasp, will look beautiful. Casual tennis shoes are fine as long as they are clean. Vivid contrasting stilettos in a smooth satin fabric will add a theatrical touch. Avoid chunky shoes and heavy wooden heels. Choose a more theatrical look, like a metallic boot or a classic loafer with a patent leather shine.

PANTS

Earth pants are best with a smooth and uncluttered front. Pant legs with a straight line will define your look. Skin tight will work surprisingly well. Flared pants can be worn with discretion in a suitable shiny material. Track pants in synthetic fabrics will convey a casual and elegant look. Jeans are best in dark and unfaded denim. Make sure the pockets are bold and neat.

PURSES & BAGS

The well-tooled classic briefcase is Earth. Try a variation on that theme for a handbag. Add elegant embroidery or a striking polished closure for a more detailed look. For casual moments carry a clutch or an oversized bag in a monochromatic color. Remember that frills will wear you down. But extraordinary beadwork will elevate your status.

JACKETS & COATS

Rock & Roll is a very Earth look. The black, the leather, the primary colors, and the metallics lend themselves well to its style. If you try a motorcycle jacket in a smooth leather, you'll likely feel at home. For business suits, keep them tailored and refined. Collars should have a well-defined line. Pockets, if any, should have strong geometry. Tuxedos are Earth. As are classic pea coats. Choose one in shiny patent leather for a modern look.

EARTH

Through Glamoury, you get there, to the diamond light.
Don your colors and shapes and shine bright.

LIGHT

For it is the 5th element of Light that creates love.
Together with the four chambers of your heart, your spirit will travel afar.

Harmony
Radiance
Resonance
Freedom
Joy

LIGHT

The element of Light is the 5th element in nature. It is the spirit that imbues everything with hope. It is the brightness that accompanies your beauty. When you are in your element, it will be with you.

Cross through the Golden Gate of Glamoury. The final step in alchemy.
A new dimension on this planet we call home. It is found within you.
Welcome home.

Love
　　Acceptance
　　　　Remembrance
　　　　　Illumination
　　　Kindness
　Forgiveness

　　　　Peace

　　　　　　　　LIGHT

Your element will take you to the magic. It will raise your vibration and create the space for the best of you to come through. These qualities of light will then infuse the world with their music. It is a power for you to understand and use.

Details for Dressing In Your Element

Using the color page, hold it up to the clothing in your closet. Look to see which page harmonizes best. Know that it is not necessary to match colors on the page. What is important is that your fashion blends into the page.

To simplify the process, you can begin with two categories. Air and Fire colors are warm and solar. Water and Earth colors are cool and lunar. If you hang all your clothing up and take a step back, you'll see.

However, keep in mind that colors sometimes sit on a border between two elements. Just like the seasons of the year, a brief blending occurs from one to the next. When this is the case, it is time to use the keywords to identify the way your clothing moves.

Color is essential, but it is even more critical that your clothing be consistent with your element's rhythm. Remember that you will be combining color, shape, and texture. Color alone will not create your look.

To identify the rhythm of your clothing, use the keywords to ask questions. For example, if you are Water, ask: Does this garment flow? Is the fabric soft? Does it blend and drape? Do I feel unrestricted?

You can also look to see if any other elements are present. Fashion is often a mix of ingredients, and this is okay. A dress that drapes and flows like Water can easily be in a color that harmonizes with Fire. If you own a dress like this, don't throw it away. Use your creativity first. Try different accessories and combinations of patterns. Ask questions using the keywords and see if it works for you.

Finally, if you don't feel at home in your element, do not be concerned. Give it time to work on you. Initially, you may not even like your element and prefer the colors and shapes of another. If this is the case, wear your element as undergarments or sleepwear and see if your opinion changes. The objective of Glamoury is transformation, so don't be afraid to try something new.

coming soon

Holding the Light, one might see
the cauldron below
in the bubbling sea.
For to hold a light as bright as love,
one must be aware of what bubbles
from below to above.

Mix and mix
the cauldron of time.
See what bubbles up,
more magic,
"The Undertone."

The undertone is a second element you will feel an
affinity to. To find out more, go to
www.glamoury.com

Kim Bieber is a daughter, mother, writer, and film producer.
Her element is Water.

9 781945 674778